HOW GOD'S GRACE AND MERCY SAVED MY LIFE

The Attitude of Gratitude

TRACY K. LEWIS

BALBOA.PRESS
A DIVISION OF HAY HOUSE

Balboa Press books may be ordered through booksellers or by contacting:

Balboa Press
A Division of Hay House
1663 Liberty Drive
Bloomington, IN 47403
www.balboapress.com
844-682-1282

Print information available on the last page.

ISBN: 978-1-9822-7308-8 (sc)
ISBN: 978-1-9822-7309-5 (e)

Balboa Press rev. date: 08/24/2021

My book is dedicated to my Mother Edna Powe
and my daughters Paige and Kayla Lewis

Life is so funny especially when you realize you don't know as much as you thought you knew. I guess that's why God said I know every thought even before you were placed in the womb, now that's what you call an awesome God. We think we have all the answers, as soon as we learn how to walk and talk and tell ourselves I can even think a little, even when I'm not for sure, that's what we call leaning unto the understanding and not understanding of God. We start telling ourselves, I can fix manage and control everything that goes wrong with myself and even want to try to fix others, but guess what happens? We make things worse than they were before we tried to step in, and fix it on our own. Well, that is what happened to me. I hit bumps, pot holes, fell in ditches and a whole lot of things that I never thought would cross my path.

See, I thought I had everything figured out but didn't have a clue about the road I was headed down. I was in the stage of wearing glasses, but not just any glasses I had on my so- called rose-colored glasses, If I only had found God sooner is what I said to myself. But guess what we can't change what is already in his plan for our lives. See here is the thing about that, God wants us to be happy in life that's why we were created in his image, but some of us get way out of control or should I say, we get big headed and we get caught up in the world of our own *(stinking thinking)*.

Me, personally have to say I'm not mad or angry at anyone for what I went through I'm grateful, thankful more than anything still here to tell my testimony because that's exactly what it is *(Thank you Lord)*. See we need to understand things that we go through in life come from the choices we make in life and it is so funny how we want to blame God when things go wrong. As long as things go our way, we are all good. Something else I realize, whenever we get ourselves of track from God, why are we so quick to say the words "the devil made me do it". *Wrong!* you made you do it, remember God gives us power, now how we choose to use it is on us, well I was one of those people who chose to want to do adventurous, curious and whatever else you want to call it, that was me and guess what I went through my own personal wakeup call from God to the point where I was on my knees begging for deliverance from all I was going through.

I was one of those people that waited until I got for the guy's y or fifty years of age to do things you do maybe when you are in your teens or maybe a little way in life, not later in life. I was one of those females that developed late in life, the kind of female that the guys didn't really look at in high school, never really had female friends, only family relatives were my friends I was not popular at all in no way. Life was rather empty for me, until I came out of so call cocoon, that's when everything started to change. I began to introduce myself to a whole new world, like Aladdin (lol)

I was surrounded by people who were well experienced, in areas of life I never even thought about that's when my whole life was changing right before my very eyes, and I'm one of those people that is going to tell my story to the point where I want to share my experiences, my strength, and the hope of never returning to that state of mind ever again. The truth is, out of everything I did I know this to be the truth... no one forced me to do anything that I did it was all my own free will (my choice) I should have been dead and gone but only by God's grace and mercy I'm still here. Doing drugs to alcohol, to performing sexual acts, from walking streets at 2:00 am, to hoping in and out of cars all times of the day and night, to working for drug dealing just to keep from being sick, to going to jail, never thought I would be there. Here is the real deal, the whole time I was doing what I was doing (God was doing what he does best). God was preparing me for something much bigger and greater, it was my purpose that he had already chose for me to do, thing was God had to let me go through what I had to go through, in order for me to be where it is he needed me to be, and do what it is he is having me to do... which is his will, not my will anymore (you will know the difference when God is using you).

All things work together for the good of those who love the Lord. I just wanted to kind of prepare your mind on a few things about me, before you actually read my story. How it all began, what I went through and how God brought me through. I never really understood the saying about... let go and let God, until I actually starting believing God, trusting God and today working more on keeping that faith. Remember we all fall short of God's glory, but here is the thing it is not about how you fall it is how you get up with God's help.

Remember....

A looser focus on what they are going through. A winner focuses on where they are going to. All men fall, but the great one's got up. Please read my book with an open mind and know that, If God brings you to it without a doubt, he will bring you through it.

I love you all with the love for our Lord and Saviour

Jesus Christ. AMEN!

Today I am blessed to be a better servant for God. A good mother, a proud grandmother, a good friend, a better Auntie, better Daughter, more responsible for my actions, more caring towards others and their feelings.

Just: *Grateful, Grateful, Grateful, Grateful*

September of 1968, when it all started for me. By the grace of God, the seed of life was placed inside of an amazing woman, whom I am very blessed to call my mother. I am the second oldest of five siblings, one sister and four brothers. My mom and dad were the type of parents that made sure as kids, we did not have to look to anyone else for anything as far as our needs, *Praise God!* We had food, shelter, clothes and other things that made my siblings and I happy. More than anything we had love. We were not wealthy or anything like that, no fancy cars and luxury homes, but we had each other and more than that we had a praying grandmother who loved Jesus, I honestly wish I had known how this man called Jesus was so amazing back when I was a child, the same man today, yesterday and forever more, but when you are a kid, your mind is on toys, cartoons and other kids just having fun being a kid.

Well, as I got older that's when my thinking started to change, now here comes my teenage years, now things are starting to look and be different to me and for me. I'm at this point in my life I want to be around older people, I want to hang out or should I say, that's when I learned some new words and those words were... (I can't wait until I am grown). Why did I say that, time rolled up on me, I had no idea what I was asking for? Now I see why people would say 'be careful what you ask for'. Now I have stepped off into being an adult, I'm feeling myself and can't nobody tell me anything, (wrong way of thinking). I was stinking thinking and did not know what I was heading for, (disaster). By now I'm starting to hang around people that were way more experience than I was, way more. I found myself going to clubs, drinking and started smoking marijuana what the kids call today "weed".

Before I go further into telling my story, which turned out to be my testimony, let me share something with you all. My parents did not do drugs; some people will say it starts in the household.... not true. I was the curious type on my own, my parents gave me more than enough love. Now, back to me being grown and curious. I was at a new phase in my life that I wanted to experience more than what I was doing, at that time for me what I was doing was not enough, something was missing (I wanted to try more). I was not what you looked at as being fine, or a super model or whatever you want to call it, I was average.

Honestly, I was more of a Tom-boy loved football, basketball things like that, hanging with the fellows. I thought boys were ok, and yes, I had a couple of guys I liked but nothing serious I was not ready to be in any type of serious relationship s with anyone, not at that time anyway. I was having too much fun at the time. So as time went on things began to start taking me in a whole new direction, by the time I reached the age of 20 years old, I met a young man, I thought to myself that maybe I am ready for a relationship, now remember how I said I was a Tom-boy meaning at that stage I had not giving myself (physically) to anyone. For some reason I felt ready with this guy, ready to be physically involved with him. That way of thinking was a mistake (Big mistake)! Anyways me and the guy went back to his place one night (he seemed really nice) by me being gullible I thought it would be ok, I was ready to give myself to him for the first time, we began to have a drink, we had good conversation, we laughed and I was enjoying that moment.

The drink was taking an effect on me and I was feeling good and warm, so we moved the conversation into the bedroom, where it was more intimate. The more we started to heat up, the more his way of thinking started to change towards me, especially when I told him this was my very first time (yes, a virgin). I had never been with a man.

As we proceeded, I guess I was not moving fast enough for him he began to get rough with me, he took my arms and held me down, he forced himself inside of me, all I could do at that moment was cry and deal with the pain. After he was done with me, he told me to hurry up and get dressed so he can take me home. As we began to drive, I noticed he went another direction than normal, see at that time we stayed not too far from each other.

I lived in Harvey and he lived in Riverdale one city over from another. I realized that we had stopped on a bridge in Riverdale, he leaned over across me opened my door and told me to get out of his car. It was 1:00 in the morning and I had to walk home. I had just been raped, I was in pain and bleeding and I was so scared. By the grace of God, I had made it home safe. That night changed my mind, I vowed never to trust another man ever. That's when my life took a turn for the worst. I had made up in my mind that I was done with men. So, I turned to women *(that was even worse)*.

Drugs and alcohol became my best friend. With drugs I didn't have to worry about feeling pain, all my pain became numb, at least for a moment. My relationship with women became even worse, I was not only being mentally and emotionally abused, I was being physically abused, the black eyes, bruised body, a knife that was put to my throat and I was kicked out all hours of the day and night. I was a total wreck, an emotional wreck, it was like I was on a roller coaster ride, back and forth, up and down, I had men and women and I had kids.

I was so confused and broken, to the point where I left my kids with my mom, and didn't care because all I knew was, Tracy wants what Tracy wanted right then and there and that's all that matters, nothing else and no one else. I stole from my youngest daughter child support checks, I sold my daughters food stamps for drugs and I would say to myself that they would be ok, it's all about me.

I went to jail working for the dope man so that I could have a supply of drugs for myself, I stole from a man who had plenty of money, I guess you can say I was a prostitute, a drug attic and an alcoholic, you name it, I did it all. The bad part about it is I did not care about how anyone felt as long as my needs and wants were being met. I was lost and out of control for years. I tried re-hab and it didn't work out for me even when I went to jail that was not enough to make me stop, not even seeing my kids hurt.

One day I told myself that I was tired and enough is enough! Rehab could not do it, so called friends could not help me, family could not help me and I began to really feel alone, lost, broken and scared until I fell to my knees, threw my hands up and called his mighty name, the one who rose with all power in his hands, the healer, deliverer, doctor, alpha omega, beginning and the end, highest, Jehovah, Lord almighty. He heard my cry and he answered, and showed up.

February 23, 2017, was when God answered my prayer, not only to be cleaned out but also cleaned up. I have not looked back since. Today I am a sponsor, and I share my testimony with others, my experience, strength and hope. The same grace and mercy God gave me; he also can give you. Just trust him, believe him. Remember he may not come when you want him to, but he is always on time.

Jesus Christ Loves me, Jesus Christ Loves you.

For who I am he forgives me of my sins and short comings, he will never leave me, he always keeps his promises, he doesn't just talk to me he listens, I am safe in his hands. No man knows the day or hour of Jesus return, the question is, will you be ready?

Before I go into the next part of my book, I want to share something with you. As you read the closing chapter of this book, please read the next few pages not only with your eyes but with your heart, your mind and your soul. It's all real because God is real, Jesus is real, the Holy Spirit is real. I want you to feel it, believe it and live it.

I pray that I may have said or even touched on something in the writing of this book that may strengthen you, encourage you and give you hope.

For God so loved the world that he gave his only begotten son, so that we should have a second chance at life. When you sit back and really think about that saying, how does that apply to you and the way you live your life? Do you ever ask yourself why would such a God like that give up his only begotten son? Well, let me give you one word to shed some light on that question for you (L.O.V.E) that word right there carries a lot of weight, especially when it is coming from the highest God, you know the one that sits high and looks low, yes, the creator of the universe.

Let me tell you a little bit about this amazing man named Jesus. When Jesus was crucified, (just because), Jesus was not crucified for the sin of you and I. Jesus life paid the price so that we would have a second chance to live, that's how much Jesus loved us. Could you imagine how God must have felt, God our father loves us so much, and Jesus the son showed you how.

John 3:16 (KJV)

God so loved the world. So, if God and Jesus did all this
for us, how do we show our love for him? Good question,
how do we?

Do we love Jesus as much as he loves us? Or do we love only what he can do for us? When we want what we want. DO we love Jesus only when we are down and sick and as soon as he takes care of our sickness, we tell him thank you but we are good, once we get back on our feet again?

Do we only love Jesus when we faced with a situation where, best friend can't fix it, not my brother, not my mother, not my sister, but only Jesus. Then once Jesus has fixed it once again, and we have made our empty promises to do better once again we are off and running, forgetting all about where my help really comes from. As we know for a fact Jesus is love always has been and always will be, but sometimes we get so caught up in everything and everyone else, until we really lose our focus on what's really important. Jesus!

Psalms 34:1 (KJV)

Bless the Lord. Now that we understood Jesus is love, and we are God's creation, how can we say we love God, or Jesus whom face we have never seen. But, we can't stand our fellow brothers or sister.

Wait! God forgave us and continues to forgive us, and we can not forgive one another, that is not love, that is our selfish pride. Pride will send us straight down that road we don't want to be on, broad and spacious. We need to remember that every saint has had a past and know that every sinner has a future, there is only one judge and that judge is the man sitting on the throne (GOD)!

Have you ever come across someone in your life, that did something wrong and you said to yourself or told someone else these words, girl I could never forgive him or her, if we take a look back over our lives, we do not have a clean track record, some even say I'm taking this to my grave? Remember God sees all and knows all.

Mark 11:25 (KJV)

Forgiveness. When we say we love God and Jesus, we have to show it, in our service to God. By doing the will of our Father who is in heaven, God knows our hearts so we have to be sincere, if we truly love him.

I never knew what love was, until I had a relationship with my savior, whom I call Jesus Christ. Forgiveness was not important to me either, but today, I can say I love Jesus, because he first loved me. God and Jesus mean more to me today than anything or anybody, and I can say that with no hesitation at all. It is a calling for me to know who my first and most important priority is Jesus.

We really need to change our way of thinking, living and way of loving because tomorrow is not promised. We need not count days, but make every day count. For something worthwhile, we may be here today because of God's grace and mercy, no one knows what the future holds but God.

1John 4:7-21 (KJV)

God is Love.

People ask the question; how do I love especially when I honestly don't know him? We have to call upon the one who gave love, the one who is love, but more than anything we call upon the one person that is the same as yesterday, today and forever more.

GOD THE FATHER

As you submit to God, he will help you to handle any situation that you say, or think is too hard for you, because guess what? Nothing is too hard for God.

Matthew 23:9 (KJV)

> God will cleanse your soul, if you call upon him for faith, trust, belief, hope, patience, endurance and remember you always have to go through the storm before you reach the calm. Let go of all bitterness, rage, anger, brawling and slander, along with every form of malice. Call on the father for cleansing.

Let me take a few moments to share with you how God works. First of all, God has no favorites, God dose have chosen ones. In other words, God has a calling on or lives. God will give you the assignments that he has chosen for you to do in life. You will know your calling by the Holy Spirit, just be still and listen. It's more than just listening there are steps you have to take before you reach your calling point.

Steps to be saved:

Mark 12:29

Hear- The lord our God is one and the only Lord *(KJV)*

John 8:24 (KJV)

Believe-For if ye believe not that I am he, ye hall die in your sins

Luke 13:3 (KJV)

Repent-I tell you nay! But unless you repent you all shall perish

Matthew 10:32 (KJV)

Confess-Whosoever confess me before man, him will I confess before my father which is in heaven

Acts 2:38 (KJV)

Baptism-Repent every one of you and be baptized in the name of Jesus for remission of your sins.

Psalms 37:23. (KJV)

Once we have taken the steps, we now are ready to walk that walk with Christ. A good man steps are ordered by the lord, and he delighted in him.

God will then begin to change your whole way of thinking, acting, loving, living because you have given up that old way of living and you have been completely transformed by God. Remember in order to receive what God has for you, you have to let go of the old and put on the new. Strip yourselves of your former nature, put off and discard your old self which characterized your previous manner of life. Remember now you're taking on a fresh mental and spiritual attitude, and you have taken on a new nature.

Ephesians 4:22-24 (KJV)

"You need to take time and look back over your life, and look how good God has been to you. Remember when those prayers went up for you. It was all God, Grace and Mercy that kept you safe and alive."

When you get a moment and you are not too busy for God, sit down in a quiet space by yourself ad really just look back over your life. Think about all you have been through, all the times you were between that rock and that hard place. The times you didn't know how you were going to pay that bill that was due, or how were you going to able to feed your family, or what about that job you wanted but they told you no. How about that position you were promised, but they gave it to someone else? What about those so-called friends that turned their backs on you, when you really thought they would be there? What about the person you confided in and they betrayed you, what about that person that you gave your heart to, and they told you these words (I won't hurt you like he did, or I won't do you like she did you). We all go through something in life that hurts us or even breaks us. Remember I life we all have to go through something before we can get to where it is God wants us to be in life, that's the key word in this story (GOD).

This is who we all need to focus on because this is the only one who can bring us through all we go through and bring us out of all we been through. God loves us so much and God has a plan for all of our lives, but here's the thing, you have to want to know your plan and purpose that God has for your life. We should be on our knees everyday shouting the words (THANK YOU JESUS). If it was not for our heavenly father, giving his son Jesus we would be so hopeless and lost. Thank God for Grace, Mercy, Love, Forgiveness, Strength and patience. Everyday God blesses you to see another day say thank you, thank him for food, clothing, shelter, family, friends, your job and transportation. Don't just count days but make every day count because you never know when your last day may be. Praise God while you can. Give thanks while you can, the time is drawing near for his return. So now, is the time we need to be preparing ourselves for Christ return. Jesus is coming whether you are ready or not!

Please don't be left behind, when the trumpet sounds, every knee shall bow, every tongue shall confess Jesus is Lord!

Here are some helpful, inspiring and encouraging words from God to strengthen you along your journey and a few words to let you know that you are not alone. Let God be your guide as you walk. All praise and Glory be to God, the Father, Son and Holy Spirit.

1. *Isaiah 54:17 (KJV)*
   No weapon formed against me shall prosper.

2. *Isaiah 3:10-11 (KJV)*
   To the righteous it shall be well with you.

3. *Romans 8:31 (KJV)*
   If God be for me, it does not matter who's against me.

4. *Psalms 37:19 (KJV)*
   Even in times of famine you will have more than enough.

5. *Isaiah 40:31 (KJV)*
   God will build you up even when situations try to bring you down.

6. *James 2:14-26 (KJV)*
   Negative energy will only make you worry but faith will make you believe.

7. *Even in your storm God will give you peace, your breakthrough is on the way.*

8. *We don't know what tomorrow may bring, so focus on the here and now.*

9. *Sin can pull you in, only when you allow it to seduce you.*

10. *Do not judge anyone, because you will be measured by the same way you judge.*

11. *Don't worry about who leaves you in life, just know that God is always there.*

12. *Holding on to someone that you need to let go of will only cause you pain.*

13.   *Leaving someone behind you, does not mean you are a bad person, it means that chapter of your life is finished.*

14.   *Stay focused on what God has in front of you, your future. Stop looking back, that's what is called the past.*

15.   *When God shows you that something is over, let it be over. Gracefully walk away.*

16.   *Please know that everyone you meet in life; is not everyone God say let in your life.*

17.   *When someone is sent from God to be in your life he will reveal things to you, through you.*

18.   *On Christ the solid rock I stand all other ground is sinking sand.*

19.   *God wants you to come to him broken, so that he may rebuild, renew and restore your faith in him.*

20.   *Never get caught up in things that are not of God, remember a moment of pleasure is not worth a life time of pain.*

21.   *Most of us have our outer sights focused on man, when we all need to have our insight focused on God.*

22.   *When we are on the war line for Christ, you better be fully suited and ready to fight. (The belt of truth, the breast plate of righteousness, Gospel of peace, shield of faith, helmet of salvation, sword of spirit).*

23.   *Church is a hospital for sick people not a museum for saints.*

24.   *When Jesus was hung, he bled and died for our sins, he paid the price and gave us the change.*

25. *It healed me, saved me and delivered me. So, I know the blood still works.*

26. *All praise and glory belong to God, praise him while you still can.*

27. *Remember what's to come is better than what has been, be patient wait on the lord.*

28. *People pleasing will cause you to lose your focus, which is God.*

29. *In order for me to keep God's word I have to give it away.*

30. *You have to go through a storm, before you can come to the calm.*

31. *It rains on the just as well as the unjust.*

32. *You can always tell when God shows up in someone life and show out because the next words, they say is... Won't he do it!!*

33. *God shows me what is worth fighting for and I will lean to your understanding and not my own.*

34. *Keep me away from anything that is not of you lord, meaning people, places or things, please guide and direct my path.*

35. *You can have all the money in the world and still be broke (Spiritually broke).*

36. *When you start to feel discouraged, call on Jesus, he will encourage you.*

37. *Have you ever heard someone say when God is ready to deliver me, he will? Well in order to be delivered you have to ask for deliverance.*

38. Stop sleeping or you will miss your blessing Gods gives everyone a wakeup call.

39. We can do any and everything man ask us to do, but as soon as God ask us to do something we respond with, why?

40. Anyone can say they love God, being obedient to his word is what he looks for.

41. When you go through rough times in life and God brings you through, you should be grateful.

42. If God brought you to it, he will definitely bring you through it.

43. When it's all said and done, the only one opinion that should matter about you is Gods, not man.

44. When God says do something don't question God, just do it.

45. Trust in the lord with all your heart. Lean not unto thy own understanding but in all thy ways acknowledge him and he will direct your path. Proverbs 3:5. **(KJV)**

46. When we ask God for something and God says no, don't get mad at God. Ask yourself what didn't I do to receive what I asked for (reality check with yourself).

47. Every situation we face in life is not a bad as we make it out to be, stop wanting to always be the victim, and start wanting to think like a victor.

48. As long as you have a broken spirit, your faith will only decrease not increase.

49. All men fall but the great ones get back up.

50. *If we pray about everything then we should not be worried about anything.*

51. *If you know what God has called you to do, stand on your calling so that God may bless you.*

52. *Remember misery loves company, so in doing Gods will there is only room for happiness, not misery.*

53. *Life is so short, so don't count days but make every day count.*

54. *If you want to see how good God's blessings are when someone tells you that you can't do it, trust in God, for courage, strength and the pleasure of knowing you can.*

55. *When God speaks to you, it will show through you, your walk, your talk and your obedience to him.*

56. *In life you can be powerful or you can be pitiful, but you can't be both, make your choice.*

57. *Before I make decisions do I talk to God, or do I decide myself and make things worse than what they were?*

58. *Do you follow or do you lead, if you put your trust in God you will lead?*

59. *For the Lord knoweth the way of the righteous, but the way of the ungodly shall perish. Psalms 1:6*

60. *Therefore, my heart is glad and my glory rejoiced, my flesh also shall rest in hope. Psalms 16:9* **(KJV)**

61. *Thou wilt shew me the path of life: In thy presence is fullness of joy, at thy right hand there are pleasures for evermore. Psalms 16:11e* **(KJV)**

62. *The Lord is my rock and my fortress and my deliverer; my God, my strength, in whom I will trust; my buckler and the horn of my salvation, and my high tower. Psalms 18:2* **(KJV)**

63. *I will call on the name of the Lord, who is worthy to be praised; so, shall I be saved from my enemies. Psalms 18:2* **(KJV)**

64. *For I have kept the ways of the lord, and have not wickedly departed from my God, Psalms 18:21* **(KJV)**

65. *As for God, his way is perfect: the word of the lord is tired; he is a buckler to all those that trust in Psalms 18:30* **(KJV)**

66. *I will bless the lord at all times; his praise will continually be in my mouth. Psalms 34:1* **(KJV)**

67. *Give instruction to a wise man, and he will be yet wiser; teach a just man, and he will increase in learning. Proverbs 9:9* **(KJV)**

68. *The heart of him that hath understanding seeketh knowledge; but the mouth of fools feedeth on foolishness. Proverbs 15:14* **(KJV)**

69. *When a man's ways please the Lord, he maketh even his enemies to be at peace with him. Proverbs 16:7* **(KJV)**

70. *A merry heart doeth God like a medicine; But a broken spirit drieth the bones. Proverbs 17:22* **(KJV)**

71. *The fear of the Lord tendeth to life: and he that hath it shall abide satisfied; he shall not be visited with evil. Proverbs 19:23* **(KJV)**

72. *He that covered his sins shall not prosper; But whosoever confessed and forsakes them shall have mercy. Proverbs 28:13* **(KJV)**

73. *But they that wait upon the Lord shall renew their strength; they shall mount up on wings as eagles; they shall run, and not be weary; they shall walk and not faint. Isaiah 40:31* **(KJV)**

74. *In six days, thou shall work, but on the seventh day thou shalt rest: in earing time and in harvest thou shall rest. Exodus 34:21* **(KJV)**

75. *The secret of the Lord is with them that fear him; and he will shew them his covenant. Psalms 25:14* **(KJV)**

76. *Look upon mine afflictions and my pain; and forgive all of my sins. Psalms 25:18* **(KJV)**

77. *Let me not be ashamed; for I put my trust in thee. Psalms 25:20* **(KJV)**

78. *Thou shall have no other Gods before me. Exodus 20:3* **(KJV)**

79. *Remember the sabbath day to keep it holy. Exodus 20:8* **(KJV)**

80. *God judgeth the righteous, and God is angry with the wicked every day. Psalms 7:11* **(KJV)**

81. *The Lord hath heard my supplications: the Lord will receive my prayer. Psalms 6:9* **(KJV)**

82. *I will praise the, O Lord with my whole heart; I will shew for all thy marvelous works. Psalms 9:1* **(KJV)**

83. *God can, and God will make a way out of no way.*

84. *Every day should be a day of thanksgiving to God, not just holidays.*

85. *The Lord is my light and my salvation; whom shall I fear; the Lord is the strength of my life; of whom shall I be afraid? Psalms 27:1* (**KJV**)

86. *The things have I desired of the Lord, that I will seek after; that I may dwell in the house of the Lord all the days of my life, to behold the beauty of the Lord, and to inquire in his temple. Psalms 27:4* (**KJV**)

87. *Deliver me not over unto the will of mine enemies: for false witnesses are risenup against me, an such as breathe out cruelty. Psalms 27:12* (**KJV**)

88. *Wait on the Lord; be of good courage and he shall strengthen thine heart; wait, I say on the Lord. Psalms 27:14* (**KJV**)

89. *The Lord is my strength and my shield; my heart trusted in him, and I am helped; therefore, my heart greatly rejoiceth; and with my song will I praise him. Psalms 28:7* (**KJV**)

90. *O love the Lord, all ye his saints: for the Lord preserveth the faithful, and plentifully rewardeth the proud doer. Psalms 31:23* (**KJV**)

91. *Keep thy tongue from evil and thy lips from speaking guile. Psalms 34:13* (**KJV**)

92. *Blessed are all they that put their trust in him. Psalms 2:12* (**KJV**)

93. *A little that a righteous man hath is better than the riches of many wicked. Psalms 37:16* (**KJV**)

94. *The steps of a good man are ordered by the Lord, and he delighted in his ways. Psalms 37:23* (**KJV**)

95. *I delight to do thy will, O my God: yea, thy law is within my heart. Psalms 40:8* (**KJV**)

96. *The fear of the Lord is the beginning of knowledge: but fools despise wisdom and instruction. Proverbs 1:7* **(KJV)**

97. *In all thy ways acknowledge him, and he shall direct thy path. Proverbs 3:6* **(KJV)**

98. *The way of the wicked is as darkness: they know not at what they stumble. Proverbs 4:19* **(KJV)**

99. *Commit thy works unto the Lord, and thy thoughts shall be established. Proverbs 16:3* **(KJV)**

100. *Better is it to be of a humble spirit with the lowly, than to divide the spoil with the proud. Proverbs 16:19* **(KJV)**

101. *The heart of the wise teacheth his mouth, and addeth learning to his lips. Proverbs 16:23* **(KJV)**

102. *Pleasant words are as a honeycomb, sweet to the soul, and health to the bones. Proverbs 16:24* **(KJV)**

103. *An ungodly man diggeth up evil, and in his lips, there is as a burning fire. Proverbs 16:27* **(KJV)**

104. *A friend loveth at all times and a brother is born for adversity. Provers 17:17* **(KJV)**

105. *He that hath knowledge spareth his words; and a man of understanding is of an excellent spirit. Proverbs 17:27* **(KJV)**

106. *The words of a man's mouth are a deep water, and the wellspring of wisdom as a flowing brook. Proverbs 18:4* **(KJV)**

107. *A man that hath friends must show himself friendly; and there is a friend thatsticketh closer than a brother. Proverbs 18:24* **(KJV)**

108. *To everything there is a season, and a time to every purpose under the heaven. Ecclesiastes 3:1* **(KJV)**

109. *Happy is the man that findeth wisdom, and the man that getteth understanding. Proverbs 3:13* **(KJV)**

110. *The lord will not suffer the soul of the righteous to famish; but he casteth away the substance of the wicked. Proverbs 10:3* **(KJV)**

111. *He that is slow to wrath is of great understanding; but he that is hasty of spirit exalteth folly. Proverbs 14:29* **(KJV)**

112. *How much better is it to get wisdom than gold; and to get understanding rather to be chosen than silver. Proverbs 16:16* **(KJV)**

113. *Judgements are prepared for scorners, and stripes for the back of fools. Proverbs 19:29* **(KJV)**

114. *Let us hear the conclusion of the whole matter: fear God and keep his commandments: for this is the whole duty of man. Ecclesiastes 12:13* **(KJV)**

115. *And also, that every man should eat and drink, and enjoy the good of all his labor, it is the gift of God. Ecclesiastes 3:13* **(KJV)**

116. *Better is a handful with quietness, than both hands full with travail and vexation of spirit. Ecclesiastes 4:6* **(KJV)**

117. *Consider the work of God; for who can make that straight, which he hath made crooked? Ecclesiastes 7:13* **(KJV)**

118. *A wise man's heart is at his right hand; but fools' heart at his left. Ecclesiastes 10:2* **(KJV)**

119. *For God shall bring every work into judgement, with every secret thing, whether it be good or whether it be evil. Ecclesiastes 12:14* (**KJV**)

120. *For I know the thoughts that I think toward you, saith the Lord, thoughts of peace, and not of evil to give you an expected end. Jeremiah 29:1* (**KJV**)

121. *Call unto me, and I will answer thee, and shew thee great and mighty things, which thou knowest not. Jeremiah 33:3* (**KJV**)

122. *But I say unto you, that ye resist not evil: but whosoever shall smite thee on thy right cheek, turn to him the other also. Matthew 5:39* (**KJV**)

123. *No man can serve two masters: for either he will hate the one, and love the other: or else he will hold to the one, and despise the other. Ye cannot serve God and money. Matthew 6:24* (**KJV**)

124. *For we brough nothing into this, and it is certain we will carry nothing out. 1Timothy 6:7* (**KJV**)

125. *And having food and raiment let us be there with content. 1Timothy 6:8* (**KJV**)

126. *But they that will be rich fall into temptation and a snare and into many foolish and hurtful lists, which drown men in destruction and perdition. 1Timothy 6:9* (**KJV**)

127. *For bodily exercise profits little: but godliness is profitable unto all things, having promise of the life that now is, and of that which is to come. 1Timothy 4:8* (**KJV**)

128. *Till I come give attendance to reading, to exhortation, to doctrine. 1Timothy 4;13* (**KJV**)

129. *Take heed unto thyself, and unto the doctrine: Continue in them: for I doing this thou shalt both save thy self, and them that hear thee. 1Timothy 4:16* (**KJV**)

130. *Fight the good fight of faith, lay hold on eternal life, where unto thou are also called, and has professed a good profession before may witnesses.*

131. *But whosoever drinketh of the water that I shall give him, shall never thirst: but the water that I shall give him shall be in him a well of water springing up into everlasting life. John 4:14* (**KJV**)

132. *132. If I have told you earthly things, and ye believe not, how shall ye believe, if I tell you of heavenly things? John 3:12* (**KJV**)

133. *He that believeth on him is not condemned: but he that believeth not is condemned already, because he hath not believed in the name of the only begotten son of God. John 3:18* (**KJV**)

134. *For every one that doeth evil hateth the light, neither cometh to the light, lest is deeds should be reproved. John 3:20* (**KJV**)

135. *For nothing is secret, that shall not be made manifest: neither anything hid, that shall not be known and come abroad. Luke8:17* (**KJV**)

136. *Those by the way side are they that hear: then cometh the devil, and taketh away the word out of their hearts, lest they should believe ad be saved. Luke 8:12* (**KJV**)

137. *I say unto you, that likewise joy shall be in heaven over one sinner that repenteth, more than over ninety and nine just persons, which need no repentance. Luke 15:7* (**KJV**)

138. *What man of you, having a hundred sheep, if he loses one of them, doth not leave the ninety and nine in the wilderness, and go after that which is lost, until he finds it. Luke 15:4* **(KJV)**

139. *Verily I say unto you, whosoever shall not receive the kingdom of God as a little child shall in no wise enter therein. Luke 18:17 (KJV)*

140. *And Jesus answering said, were there not ten cleansed? But where are the nine? There are not found that returned to give glory to God, save this stranger. Luke 17:17-18 (KJV)*

141. *Then Jesus said, Father forgive them: for they know not what they do, and they parted his raiment, and cast lots. Luke 23:34* **(KJV)**

142. *And he saith unto them, why are ye fearful, O ye of little faith? Matthew 8:26* **(KJV)**

143. *Ask and it shall be given you: seek and ye shall find: knock and it shall be opened unto you. Matthew 7:7* **(KJV)**

144. *He that loveth father or mother more than me is not worthy of me: and he that loveth son or daughter more than me is not worthy of me. Matthew 10:37* **(KJV)**

145. *Come unto me, all ye that labor and are heavy laden, and I will give you rest. Matthew 11:28* **(KJV)**

146. *No weapon formed against me shall prosper. Isaiah 54:17* **(KJV)**

147. *I waited patiently for the Lord; and he inclined unto me, and heard my cry. Psalms 40:1* **(KJV)**

148. *I said, I will take heed to my ways, that I sin not with my tongue; I will keep my mouth with a bridle, while the wicked is before me. Psalms 39:1* **(KJV)**

149. *And the Lord shall help them, and deliver them: he shall deliver them from the wicked, and save them, because they trust in him. Psalms 37:40* **(KJV)**

150. *I delight to do thy will, O my God; yea, the law is within my heart. Psalms 40:8* **(KJV)**

151. *God is our refuge and strength, a very present help in trouble. Psalms 46:1* **(KJV)**

152. *Cause me to hear thy loving kindness in the morning; for in thee do I trust: cause me to know the way where I should walk; for I lift up my soul unto thee. Psalms 143:8* **(KJV)**

153. *Search me. O God, and know my heart: try me and know my thoughts; and see if there be any wicked way in me, and lead me in the way everlasting. Psalms 39:23-24* **(KJV)**

154. *The Lord is gracious, and full of compassion: slow to anger, and of great mercy. Psalms 144:8* **(KJV)**

155. *Happy is that people, that is in such a case: yea happy is that people, whose God is the Lord. Psalms 144:15* **(KJV)**

156. *The Lord is righteous I all his ways, and holy in all his works. Psalms 145:17* **(KJV)**

157. *The Lord preserveth all them that love him: but all the wicked will he destroy. Psalms 145:20* **(KJV)**

158. *My mouth shall speak the praise of the Lord: and let all flesh bless his holy name for ever and ever. Psalms 145:21* **(KJV)**

159. *But I say unto you, love your enemies, bless them that curse you, do good to them that hate you, and pray for them which despitefully use you, and persecute you. Matthew 5:44* **(KJV)**

160. *And behold a woman which was diseased with an issue of blood twelve years, came behind him and touched the hem of his garment. Matthew 9:20* **(KJV)**

161. *For she said within herself, if I may but touch his garment, I shall be whole. Matthew 9:21 (KJV)*

162. *For whosoever shall do the will of my father which is in heaven, the same is my brother, and sister and mother. Matthew 12:50 (KJV)*

163. *This I say then, walk in the spirit and ye shall not fulfill the lust of the flesh. Galatians 5:16 (KJV)*

164. *Now the works of the flesh are manifest, which are this adultery, fornication, uncleanness, lasciviousness. Galatians 5:19 (KJV)*

165. *Idolatry, witchcraft, hatred, variance, emulations, wrath, strife, sedations, heresies. Galatians 5:20 (KJV)*

166. *Envying, murders, drunkenness retellings, and such like: of the which I tell you before, as I have also told you in time past, that they which do such things shall not inherit the kingdom of God. Galatians 5:21 (KJV)*

167. *Faith is the substance of things hoped evidence of things not seen. Hebrews 11:1 (KJV)*

168. *We don't know what the future holds, but we do know who holds the future.*

169. *For God so loved the world that he gave his only begotten son, that whosoever believeth in him shall not perish but have everlasting life. John 3:16 (KJV)*

Before I close out my book here are a few thoughts that I thought would be helpful and also give you strength while you continue your walk with Christ. Be blessed, be safe and always put God first, he is the way, truth and the light.

1) *Don't use your energy to worry, use your energy to believe.*

2) *Stay in peace, because your about to walk into your season.*

3) *Your destiny is not tied to those who walk away from you, it's tied to God whom is always there for you.*

4) *Whatever relationships God want you to have he will provide, that's when you know it's of God's doing and not man's.*

5) *Every sinner has a future and every saint has a past all have sinned and fallen short of God's glory.*

6) *Jesus paid the price and gave us the change, when he hung, and died on the cross for our sins.*

7) *It healed me, saved me and delivered me, so I know it still works the blood of Jesus.*

8) *I don't have to wait till I see him, I'm going to praise him now because I believe him.*

9) *Love was not just put in your heart just for a day, love is only real when you give it away.*

10) *What's to come is better than what has been.*

11) *People pleasing has caused us to neglect what's most important, God's work and word.*

12) *In order for me to keep God's words in myself I have to give it away to others.*

13) *In life you have to go through your storm before you get to the calm.*

14) *Rain falls on the just as well as the unjust.*

15) *Help me to steer clear of relationships that lead me away from the path (God), you have laid out for me.*

16) *When people try to discourage you, stay close to God, he will encourage you.*

17) *Stop sleeping or you will dream right through your blessing, God gives everyone a wakeup call.*

18) *We can do any and everything man ask us to do but as soon as God ask something of us our response is Why? Don't question God just do it.*

19) *Anyone can say they love God but being obedient to his word is what he looks at.*

20) *When you go through tough times in life and God brings you through, you should have the attitude for gratitude.*

21) *If God brought you to it, he will definitely bring you through it.*

22) *You may be down and thinking you're out but God never gives up on us he is the same God yesterday, today and forever more.*

23) *If you don't stand for something in life you will fall for anything (stand for Christ).*

24) *Everyone wants to go to heaven but does not want to do the work that it is going to take to get there.*

25) *If you put God first in everything and all things you will never be last in his sight.*

26) *God already knows what it is your trying to figure out, but prayer helps you to work it out.*

27) *When we pray, we need not worry, if we worry why are we praying (oh yea of little faith).*

28) *God has a plan for everyone, but your plan can't be blessed if we don't trust in him.*

29) *When we are doing God's will, happiness usually is the result of being too busy to be miserable.*

30) *Sometimes in life people will tell you that you will not amount to anything, prove them wrong tell them that's not what God's plan shows you.*

31) *Don't count days in life but make every day count for something meaningful, especially to God.*

32) *In life you can be pitiful or powerful but you cannot be both.*

33) *Faith is not built on your circumstances; your faith is built on God's trust.*

34) No matter what I go through on a daily basis, as long as I trust in God it will all be ok.

35) I can't make any decisions without asking God for guidance upon it.

36) Do you want to follow people of the world? Or do you want to lead souls to Christ? Stay diligent in his word, you will surely lead.

37) In life it is better to be with no one than it is to be with the wrong one. Wait on God he knows what is best.

38) Be careful how you treat a stranger you never know when you're in the company of an angel.

39) Stop looking behind you, because you will miss what God has in front of you, let your past be your past.

40) Do we look for reasons to doubt Gods promises? Or a reason to believe him?

41) If you keep doing the same things over and over and the results never change then maybe you should make a change and try God.

42) Sometimes we can make a permanent decision over a temporary situation, think before you act (Pray).

43) Misery never has to be alone because company is not too far behind.

44) Nothing is more powerful than when you want to have a changed mind, focusing on Christ.

45) It is a very short trip to hell, but a wonderful journey to heaven.

46) *The fear of the lord is the beginning of wisdom, wise are those that fear the Lord.*

47) *Step up to God's growth chart and measure your progress.*

48) *Sometimes in life God has to delay your blessings, that does not mean you're being denied of them, wait on the Lord.*

49) *Stop doing what others think is important, and do what is urgent to God (his will).*

50) *You need to know that sometimes we don't know enough, God is the only one that knows it all.*

51) *We should never interrupt someone that is doing what we said could not be done (God said all things are possible through him). Won't he do it!!!*

52) *The devil wants you to stay focused on your past, but God says keep your eyes on me, I am your future.*

53) *God says we are not slow to learn we are just quick to forget.*

54) *Eyes have not seen ears have not heard, that's what it feels like when you desire God deep down in your soul.*

55) *Lord I ask with all that I have and all that I am I give myself away so you can use me according to your will.*

56) *To wait on the Lord is to have rest in the Lord, stay focused on God.*

57) *When you are in God's waiting room, don't worry it won't be long, because God has the prescription you have been waiting on.*

58) *Lord give me the taste for righteousness and the distaste for sin.*

59) *God gave us people to love, and days to use, but we turn things around for the opposite. We love days and use people.*

60) *The bible says a good woman is worth more than diamonds, she senses the worth of her work and is in no hurry to call it quits.*

61) *In the midst of a crisis feelings run wild don't be quick to make a decision in your storm.*

62) *God will forgive you but he doesn't want you repeating the same cycle over and over of the same sin.*

63) *God doesn't respond to need; he responds to faith so seek your faith on his unbreakable word and stand on his promise.*

64) *Your mind will always believe everything you tell it, feed it hope, feed it truth, feed it love, trust God.*

65) *The extent of my serenity will determine the quality of my life.*

66) *If you focus on results, you will never see change, but if you focus on change you will see results.*

67) *You have to know your problem before you can find a solution, call upon God in prayer he has the answer.*

68) *We repeat what we don't repair, so make the repairs so that it will not be repeated.*

69) *Listen to learn, so that you may better hear when you listen.*

70) *You can't change everything you are faced with, but once you face those things you can make a change.*

As I now come to a close of this chapter of my life I pray and hope that I have shared something with you that may help you. If you are going through what I have been through or you may be going through a storm at this very moment, please be encouraged to know that God has no spectators. God will also give you Grace and Mercy that he gave me. It was not an easy road for me to take to get to where it I that I am at this point in my life. It was stressful, painful, and to resist the light of temptation I had to let go of a lot of people that were no longer good for me. I had to remove myself from places that I knew were no longer good for me. To make it in life we have to go through a storm before we can come to the calm in our lives. God is so good; God never has changed he is the same God today, yesterday and forever more, I was the one always walking away from God, because I never trusted in God like I should have, never studied his word as I do today never have a relationship with him like I have now, never knew I would love Jesus the way that I do today he is truly my rock, my help, my comforter, my prescription, my strength when I am weak. I have never thanked God as much as I thank him today, more grateful than I have ever been, more willing to want to do his will and no longer trying to do self-will, so I pray that my experience, strength and hope will give you encouragement and not discouragement. Remember and please know God is real and that Jesus loves you so much that he died for you and me. Here are some scriptures for inspiration apply them to your daily life.

Matthew 6:33 (KJV)

Matthew 6:24 (KJV)

Mark 8:36 (KJV)

Luke 2:52 (KJV)

John 4:24 (KJV)

Romans 8:28 (KJV)

Romans 10:17 (KJV)

Galatians 6:9 (KJV)

Hebrews 4:12 (KJV)

Revelations 22:12 (KJV)

Psalms 51:10 (KJV)

Isaiah 40:31 (KJV)

Jeremiah 29:11 (KJV)

Songs of inspiration don't just listen to the songs hear the words and what they mean.

James Fortune – *I trust you*

Shekinah Glory Ministry – *Praise is what I do*

Paul Jones – *I won't complain*

Tim Bowman Jr. – *I'm good*

Malcom Williams – *The blood still work Chicago Mass Choir-God is my everything*

Evvie McKinney – *Ain't that just like God Shirley Ceasar-Your next in line for a miracle*

Songs that will inspire you when you feel like all faith, hope, trust and love is gone.

1. *Smokie Norful – Still Say Thank You*

2. *Fred Hammond – Be a Fence*

3. *Tasha Cobb – Getting Ready*

4. *Jekalyn Carr – Greater is Coming*

5. *New York Restoration – Speak to My Heart*

6. *Anthony Brown – Trust in You*

7. *Lemme Battles – You're Looking at A Miracle*

8. *Marvin Sapp – My Testimony*

AUTOBIOGRAPHY

I was born on September 16th, 1968 in Chicago, Illinois, to Edna J. Lewis. We lived on the south side of Chicago. In 1969 my mother met the love of her life Lymon Powe who became a big part of my life. We moved around a lot when I was younger, as my family grew, we settled down in Harvey, Illinois where I now reside. I have been in few places and have come across a lot of people. But nothing is greater than where I am now, I am living in Christ, I have come to know an amazing savior, and I have met an amazing, the great I am, all mighty King and his name is Jesus!!! I am exactly where God wants me to be. All Praise and Glory be to God!!

THANKS

All praise and thanks go to my highest power, whom I call God, for blessing me to be able to tell my story of how grateful I am for having his son Jesus Christ not only for dying for my sins but how grateful I am, Jesus Christ delivered me from drugs, alcohol, cigarettes and all of things that are not of God. I thank my daughters Paige Lewis and Kayla Lewis for not giving up on me even when I wanted to give up on myself. I thank my youngest brother Brucey Powe for being tough on me when I was so lost and weak. I thank God for blessing me with a wonderful mother, an amazing dad and four other siblings. I thank Kesha for always being there for me when I needed her the most. I never realized just how much I valued life until I realized I could have been dead sleeping in my grave, but through all I went through God kept me here. I knew what my calling was, but was not ready to answer to it. but I never knew my talents until the Holy Spirit led me right to it. I am using it to tell my Testimony of what God has shown me, before he could let me be who I am today.

Why do I love Jesus? Well, that question is not hard to answer for me.

When they nailed him to the cross our sins were washed away completely sin free.

Even through the torture he suffered before he hung his head and died just to see the abuse, he took for me all mankind should make us feel some type of way deep down inside.

Jesus even cried out to his father, saying forgive them for they know not what they do.

How many of us honestly can say, that we could have taken the type of pain that Jesus went through.

When I think about all that God has done for me, the only reason I am still here is because of his grace love and mercy. We all fall short and sin in some type of way, that is why we have to confess our sins to God and pray, pray, pray.

I won't sit here and tell you that everything I went through; God took it all away overnight.

I had a whole lot of work to do and yes, the devil stayed on me it was a fight.

I had to go, to God broken on bended knee, threw my hands in the air and said here I am please deliver me.

Walking by faith and not by sight, victory is what I was receiving from God, and all his might.

All you have to do is have faith the size of a mustard seed, nothing is too hard for our God, absolutely nothing indeed. If God, did it for me, he can do it for you, just get out of the way and get ready for your break through.

I'm going to be honest with all, when I was in the streets it was like being in the pit of hell.

Matter a fact I felt like Jonah in the bible when he was stuck in the belly of the whale.

See God gives everyone a wakeup call some may wake up quick, some may not wake up at all.

Every day that God bless you to wake up and be here, you should fall to your knees, because no one knows the time, day or hour but the lord is drawing near.

That is why we have stay strong in Jesus no matter what may come or what may be.

Jesus paid the price and gave us the change, even in the midst of my nonsense Jesus never gave up on me.

I don't know how much pain a person has to go through to say ok I have learned some lessons.

Don't you want to be joyful, happy and free, if so, let's go get these blessings.

Don't worry about how people are going to look at you, or what they are going to say.

See once you give your life to Christ, guess what take one step, Christ is going to take two now you are on your own way.

Don't you want to live with Christ in heaven for eternity.

Or do you want to hear the words from Jesus saying depart from me.

I pray that something in my book may have touched you. Please remember always to thy own self be true. Know that I love you, but God loves you even more. So much that he died for all mankind.

Jesus died for me. So I must live for him.

CPSIA information can be obtained
at www.ICGtesting.com
Printed in the USA
BVHW080033240921
617451BV00002B/74